Rare Treasure of Destiny

Medication for the Nations

Revolutionary Spiritual Remedies for a World in Crisis

Rare Treasure of Destiny

Smyrna's Spiritual Specialist

Stan Conely

&

Tommie Howard

RESOURCE *Publications* · Eugene, Oregon

RARE TREASURE OF DESTINY

Smyrna's Spiritual Specialist

Copyright © 2013 Stan Conely and Tommie Howard. All rights reserved. Except for brief quotations in critical publications or reviews, no part of this book may be reproduced in any manner without prior written permission from the publisher. Write: Permissions, Wipf and Stock Publishers, 199 W. 8th Ave., Suite 3, Eugene, OR 97401.

Resource Publications

An Imprint of Wipf and Stock Publishers

199 W. 8th Ave., Suite 3

Eugene, OR 97401

www.wipfandstock.com

ISBN 13: 978-1-62032-816-3

"Scripture quotations taken from the New American Standard Bible®,
Copyright © 1960, 1962, 1963, 1968, 1971, 1972, 1973,
 1975, 1977, 1995 by The Lockman Foundation
Used by permission." (www.Lockman.org)

Manufactured in the U.S.A.

To my wife, Rochelle:

Your patience, understanding, sacrifices, support, and encouragement strengthen my spirit every day. No other project is more important to me than striving to be the man you will always want and need. Thank you for being a special companion, confidant, helper, and treasure.

Stan

I dedicate this book for my friend and brother in Christ, Stan Conely who's dedication and passion for the work of service knows no limits. I also lovingly dedicate this book to my family on earth and in heaven for the sacrificial support that I have been given to endure the rigors of Christian service over the years.

Tommie

Contents

Preface | **viii**

Acknowledgments | **xii**

INTRODUCTION TO THE SERIES

Overview | **1**

A Proven Healing Process | **4**

Beyond Reading | **9**

NOTHING LIKE THE REAL THING

Critical Life Events | **15**

    Devotion 1: Challenge Reflections | **20**

    Devotion 2: The Bible as a Guide | **21**

Last One Standing | **25**

    Devotion 3: In the Mind of God | **30**

    Devotion 4: Uniquely Focused | **32**

Powerless Philosophies | **34**

Devotion 5: Rescue Option | **38**

The Cost of Acceptance | **41**

Devotion 6: Seeking Approval | **46**

DESTINED FOR EACH OTHER

Directions of Fulfillment | **51**

Devotion 7: Navigation Necessities | **62**

What's the plan, here? | **65**

Devotion 8: Researching Renewal | **69**

Devotion 9: Specialized Selections | **72**

Devotion 10: Fortunes of Fascination | **80**

Exhibit E – Experience | **84**

Devotion 11: Answering the Call | **91**

Devotion 12: Evidently Present | **98**

Notes | **105**

Literature on the Bible | **109**

Preface

IT IS NO SECRET THAT SINCE THE UNITED STATES '08 financial crash; western economies (relying on the US) have been in perpetual anxiety, and like a virus it has infected the entire globe. The interdependence of the world is so much smaller than in previous centuries that the disintegration of merely one country can push the entire globe to the edge of cyclical implosion. Mass demonstrations have been springing up around the globe with social media being used as tactical tools for class warfare rather than relational luxuries by quirky adolescents. Global leaders have frantically made split decisions to abate roaring rebellions against their stagnant conditions, the likes of which history has never seen before. As with all turbulent periods of human history, spiritual leaders have continually trumpeted that the end of the world is near and that certain tools are needed to survive our difficult circumstances.

However, what fails to be communicated by many spiritual leaders is that our global crisis is not the one we hear in the media of the repeated seesaw fluctuations of the world's markets. The problems in our society do not truly hinge on the hostile finger pointing between the rich and the poor. The true crisis as an ancient spiritualist forwarned us almost 2000 years ago lies in the painful vanity of men attempting to control what men have never and will never be able to control, *"the future"*. If you are fearful of the Dow-Jones Industrial average or cringe with nervous expectation over the next statistical findings on the trends of the next monitory devaluation; then I urge you to hear the words of the universal wisdom of the greatest world leader of all time, *". . . I understand your anxieties and the humiliation of your poverty, but you are wealthy . . ."*[1] *(Jesus of Nazareth 59 AD)*.

THE MESSAGE OF THE GREATEST SPIRITUALIST
THE WORLD HAS EVER KNOWN

Whether it is Buddha or Mohammed, the lessons of Shiva or the Zoroaster, spiritual communication transcends reason and rational speculation. This is because the unseen essence of human beings strives to connect with that which gives it comfort and security. It is undeniable that men, women and children will defy the forces of nature itself to cling to the completeness they experience when their spiritual essence has been completed. Critics of this human need such as Karl Marx described it as "... *Religion is the opium of the people...*"[2]. Unknowingly however, even Marx was a Spiritualist because he also appealed to the need of his followers to fill an essential drive for purpose and meaning in their human existence.

It is undeniable that Jesus of Nazareth is the greatest spiritualist the world has ever known. Even though his physical time on earth was merely a glimpse of human history (approximately 33 years), his teachings can be found in the lives of people in every corner of the planet, and continue to maintain the evolutionary force to endure the duration of man's universal existence. Emperors, Kings, Rulers, Conquerors and Presidents continually recite his transcending wisdom to govern their very societies and capture the confidence of the masses of those who have never even seen or understand him. This is because the wisdom of a spiritualist descends from beyond this earth, with teachings the nature of which connects with the deepest part of us, filling us with a perspective beyond our natural existence.

Acknowledgments

No one knows me as intimately as my Savior. He's mainly responsible for this work, and I'm humbled to be used as His vessel. The powerful influence of my two loving parents who've nurtured me in the Lord can never be stressed enough; and my passion for spirituality stems from the genuine love of my very close family, relatives, and friends. I will forever be indebted to my Creator for the gifts that are my wife and children. They've taught me much more about life than I ever could've learned from any formal training. Also, to everyone at *Wipf & Stock Publishing*, you've been unbelievably accommodating in helping to make this vision a reality. And, finally, to my brothers and sisters in Fort Wayne, Indianapolis, Demotte, Muncie, and Houston – you know who you are – your encouragement, prayers, and cultivation have shaped me immensely. Wherever you are, I know God's using you to do His work. May He bless and keep you until that day.

Stan

To Southwestern Christian College, the late James W. Fergason, Abilene Christian University and my brothers and sisters in Christ

Tommie

Introduction to the Series

OVERVIEW

You won't have to search long or hard to find headlines of disturbing events that rock and shatter communities to their very core. Crime, greed, civil war, slavery, and violence are just a few examples of the harsh realities present in our world. And these don't even include the plethora of injustices and difficulties people encounter that go unreported every day. Those who are overwhelmed with the obstacles of life sometimes resort to destructive coping mechanisms like alcoholism or illegal substances. Others endure lives of quiet desperation in abusive and hurtful relationships hoping that things will eventually make a turn for the better, but oftentimes they do not. Fortunes are spent attempting – often unsuccessfully – to find the rationale or remedy for depression; while many who contemplate suicide believe that love and acceptance will never be anything more than a distant fantasy. Some would even destroy themselves and others desperately seeking ways to find satisfaction in life only to discover the emptiness of short-lived pleasures in their quest. When considering these sorts of challenges and complications in our world, no one should be surprised at the astronomical amount of time and energy society places on finding viable solutions for these universal struggles? But so many efforts to resolve humanity's issues seem to frequently fall short of producing consistent and sustained healing. This often breeds greater disappointment and more discouragement, which only fuels our desires to solve those complexities in life that so easily and routinely perplex us.

To eliminate the guess work and theorizing of what can actually help humanity, *Medication for the Nations: Revolutionary Spiritual Remedies for a World in Crisis*, sets itself apart as a panacea for generating the kind of change that can correct and even reverse so many destructive societal trends. By using one of the most unique texts in scripture as a guide, this multi-volume inspirational series takes readers on a journey of discovering how purpose, progress, and true fulfillment can only be achieved through establishing a close relationship with the Creator and understanding His will for our lives. While new and creative methods for tackling common ills of the human experience are brought to light, a perfect and accessible remedy for the source behind most of humanity's problems is explored and revealed. Lending itself to this quest is a very unique section of scripture found in the book of Revelation that shows Jesus communicating a message of exceptional insight to seven distinct and diverse church communities in Asia. Throughout His address, a magnificent pattern surfaces that sets the premise and foundation for this series by presenting Jesus as an expert spiritual physician who carefully examines and creatively treats the illnesses of a spiritually sick people in need of His rare talents and unparalleled guidance. More broadly, this series investigates how many issues associated with the church often originate from the broader context of the community in which the church exists. In fact, it is that very reciprocal relationship of the world and the church that this series seeks to thoroughly inspect – how the world can negatively affect the church and how the church is designed to positively affect the world. In the end, spiritual growth and maturity are recognized as the keys for implementing effective individual and collective change; and readers are able to measure how their own spiritual condition compares with the Creator's standard of what true spiritual development looks like and how it is maintained.

A PROVEN HEALING PROCESS

Perhaps, the greatest feature of *Medication for the Nations* can be found in the creative four-volume approach used for each of the seven communities addressed. This method resembles the steps of an effective healing process from diagnosis to recovery and analyzes each community in four separate volumes that break down into following themes:

1. ***The Spiritual Specialist***: As a masterful specialist, Jesus describes Himself in a way that tailors to the specific needs of each church's situation and society, in general.

2. ***The Spiritual Exam***: Being a skilled spiritual examiner, Christ identifies the intricate qualities and any shortcomings of each individual church and society's larger influence on it.

3. ***Spiritual Injections***: With unmatched expertise in the area of spiritual treatment, the Messiah reveals practical and insightful solutions for successfully meeting the Creator's high expectations for spiritual maturity.

4. ***Spiritual Incentives***: The Master offers a realistic glimpse of the Christian's spiritual reward as motivation for those who stay the course and endure the spiritual race.

Themes in *The Spiritual Specialist* volumes cover a full spectrum of qualities and attributes associated with Jesus. On the one hand, Christ is painted as someone who possesses authority extending beyond the natural boundaries of this world; but another very intimate portrait is also emphasized as a man who can relate very closely with the woes and troubles of the human condition. He is esteemed as an individual like no other in the history of mankind by not only pointing out His distinctive role when compared to other world-wide religious leaders of the past and present, but by also stressing His part in

Introduction

humanity's plan for intimacy with the Creator. With unmatched experience from Christ's divine nature, His unprecedented ability to correct destructive tendencies, and resources that assist with the maintenance of moral and ethical practices; these volumes lead and empower the reader to set a standard with which to develop spiritually that is both flawless and unequaled.

The Spiritual Exam seeks to highlight the benefits of all those qualities Jesus commends in his address to the seven churches of Asia while, at the same time, warning against the detrimental effects of those characteristics He despises. When looking at these assessments from the broader context of society, the reader begins to discover how effective Christ's counsel and wisdom can be as it can be applied to any human context. Themes addressed in these volumes include but are not limited to the following topics: integrity, social acceptance, spiritual complacency, poverty, enduring persecution, hypocrisy, steadfastness in the midst of corruption, and assessing the legitimacy of spiritual leaders and teaching. Eventually, readers come to discover how crucial it is to place a high priority on mastering the kind of behaviors, thoughts and speech that Jesus not only encouraged, but also modeled, Himself.

Spiritual Injections are exactly that - distinguishing doses of spiritual medicine for each of the very different communities Jesus addressed. As someone who understands the fine and intricate details of what it takes to live godly and thrive spiritually, Christ divulges simple yet profound solutions for a number of human woes that – directly or indirectly – plague society. These volumes are so effective because challenges that face the church frequently mirror difficulties of the world community. Topics in these sections focus on spiritual revival, achieving true sustained repentance, overcoming fears, increasing courage, handling negative peer pressure, developing genuine humility, improved discipline, heightened motivation, spiritual wisdom, and sacrificial living. These treasures of knowledge offered by Jesus were – from the very beginning of time – designed to bring about healing and more abundant living to all who practice them. And readers come to realize that all who flourish in these remedies equip themselves to successfully tackle the challenging obstacles life can present.

Spiritual Incentives delve into some of the extraordinary benefits associated with spiritual maturity. More specifically, these volumes are designed to be a motivating factor for all who remain consistent in striving for that standard of living set by the Creator. Characterized by an in-depth exploration of how Jesus ends His address to each of the church communities in Asia, He expounds on topics such as life after death, immortality, the Creator's deliverance, protection, guidance, and direction. Emphasis is placed on all the advantages that are available to God's followers; and attention is drawn to how there is a uniquely designed purpose for the church, collectively, and each person, individually. Only, that purpose can neither be realized nor completely discovered without coming to accept the Creator's will.

BEYOND READING

Complementing the distinctive four-volume approach of *Medication for the Nations* is a number of meticulously designed *devotional activities* that supplement each volume. These activities were developed with a very ambitious agenda to model the kind of elements Christ used that made His teaching so attractive and effective. Jesus taught and ministered in ways that were brilliantly profound yet amazingly simplistic; and His ability to stimulate others toward spiritual growth across all human spectrums conveys an essence that is clearly rooted in divine origins. In a similar fashion, devotions throughout this series were conceived with both individual and collective spiritual development in mind. The versatility of each activity can help facilitate productive moments of personal meditation while generating exceptional small and large study group applications, at the same time. These activities are meant to perpetuate the kind of discussion and reflection that help readers connect with the topics addressed in very personal ways and seek to accommodate the needs

Introduction

of both novice learners and experienced scholars, alike. In fact, it is a foregone conclusion that some who read this series may not even be familiar with or accepting of the Bible's credibility. One of many goals, then, is to establish the legitimacy and uniqueness of scripture, which will not only solidify the faith of Bible believers, but hopefully alleviate the doubts of Bible skeptics, as well.

From the busiest metropolis to the most remote village in the countryside and everywhere else in between, people from all corners of our planet yearn internally for the kind of guidance that can only be provided by the Creator. One biblical prophet, Jeremiah, even wrote to this point in scripture with these words, *"I know, O Lord, that a man's life is not his own; it is not for man to direct his steps."(Jeremiah 10:23).* While some may completely suppress the reality of this need, attempting to consistently navigate our own direction alone is limited to destinations of emptiness and can only lead to an unfulfilled state of existence. The burning question, then, for this generation – and any before or after it – involves determining

God's will and purpose for humanity. Interestingly, it is this very same Creator who continuously directs us to Christ as having all the keys to achieving true wholeness and fulfillment. But how do we access the wisdom and insight of someone who no longer exists on this earth physically? Some have argued that if only Christ could speak to us today as clearly and directly as He did with people in the Bible long ago, the church – and world, for that matter – would be in a much better place. Congregations would be stronger, neighborhoods less violent, families not as dysfunctional, and individuals more spiritual. What too many people fail to realize, though, is that our Creator gives us direction and guidance today that is just as powerful as any other time in human history. *Medication for the Nations* proves this point by not only providing a flawless measure and penetrating mirror for consistent spiritual growth, but by also rendering modern applications of Christ's life-changing words that transcend both time and culture – to His followers and for anyone else who would hear.

Introduction

SECTION ONE

Nothing Like The Real Thing

Critical Life Events

A FEW SPRINGS AGO SOME TORNADOES RIPPED through the city and vicinity where we lived. My family and I were living in a two-story house with no basement, and so the safest place to ride out the storm was the lower-level bathroom located near the center of the house. You can always tell when the weather's getting worse. Light bulbs begin to flicker, the rain gets stronger, lightning makes the night sky look like day, and it feels like thunder will shatter the windows at any second. Within an instant, all power in the house completely died; and we began the safety routine it felt like we had been practicing, at least, twice a week for about a month. Pillows, blankets, flashlights, snacks, drinks, and a power generating radio all got crammed into the half bathroom, along with our family of five. When the initial power outage occurred, chaos ensued. It was so dark we couldn't see right in front of us. My daughters began crying and asking where everybody was. My son was just as scared, but hid his emotions a little better by trying to reassure his sisters. After hearing the calm voice of their mother, the children searched their way through the darkness to the sofa where she was. "It's OK," she said, "I'm sure your father will have the flashlight in just a moment." But her words were more than just a statement. There was a tone of urgency in her voice and a little nervousness, as well.

My job had always been the same in a situation like this – get to a flashlight, and assist with getting everyone (and everything) into the bathroom as quickly as possible. Unfortunately, sometimes the actual event doesn't go as smoothly as the drill. Searching through the darkness in previous experiences like this made for a lot of broken flashlights. Not on purpose, though. When you can't see, it can be easy to accidentally knock a flashlight over or drop it on the ground. And even if you have a general idea of where it is, you can carelessly hit it with another object while trying to find your way through pitch blackness. In the worst case scenario, the flashlight breaks. This can be caused by any number of things – a busted light bulb, cracked lens, or something internal malfunctioning, for example. But at such a critically important time, when my family was huddled on a sofa fearing the possibility of a tornado striking the house, I had learned better than to just depend on any flashlight. It had to be special, reliable, durable, and long lasting. One I could trust to do its job when my family and I needed it the most.

Years earlier when I was deployed oversees, my first sergeant was the initial person to show me this flashlight. Having had so many die out on me at critical times makes his words ring out that much more loudly and clearly in my mind today. "I've been around for quite a while, sergeant," he said confidently. "Now, I don't claim to know everything, but I know a lot. And, you won't find a better flashlight than this one right here. It'll be the first and last one you ever need!" He gave it to me brand new, but you wouldn't have believed his words by simply looking at it. Small and extremely heavy for its size, nothing about it came across as particularly special. In fact, its appearance alone would have rendered it somewhat insignificant. But when the light turned on, it was, at least, three times brighter and stronger than any flashlight I'd ever seen. To this day, I've never had to change or replace anything on it – even though there's a compartment on its case with extra parts, should the need ever arise. Once, I even witnessed it get accidentally dropped down two flights of stairs onto solid concrete and turn right on without even a weakening flicker. It requires a special light bulb, has a special battery, and is made with a very special material. What else would I use to navigate through the darkness and help my family to safety? I've found no other to do what it does, none so trustworthy to provide light when it's so critically important, and refuse to settle for anything less. Nothing can compare to it, and my complete confidence lies within it – the real thing.

When it comes to spirituality, having the real thing is just as essential, and even more so. We simply can't afford to depend on just anything or anyone, but some are willing to take that risk. Our spiritual survival, however, is much too critical a thing to leave to chance! *The instinctive need within us all seeks to be connected with someone who can help provide direction at unclear times and will be completely reliable, especially during the most trying moments of our existence here on this earth.* But how can we know who or what is reliable? And where do we even begin searching for answers? Perhaps, a great place to start is by exploring the most widely used and printed spiritual writing in mankind's history – the Bible. While there have been many to doubt its authenticity and question its legitimacy, it has still remained universally accepted and reliable by people from a variety of different cultures, educational backgrounds, socio-economic levels, and geographic locations. Time will be spent, at length, discovering why this is throughout different sections of this series. But for our current task, at least, entertain the possibility that *the Bible not only offers some very unique insights into our human nature, but also has the potential to open our minds to the kind of guidance and purpose in life that many of us so passionately seek.*

Devotion 1: Challenge Reflections

> *"The instinctive need within us all seeks to be connected with someone who can help provide direction at unclear times and will be completely reliable, especially during the most trying moments of our existence here on this earth."*

*Take a moment to reflect on and respond to the statement and questions below.

Statement	Question 1	Question 2
Create a list of a few obstacles or challenges you currently face.	Who do you think might be able to help you cope with or overcome these challenges? Why this person (or these people)?	What do you think could be done to help you deal with these obstacles?
Challenge 1: ⇨		⇨
Challenge 2: ⇨		⇨
Challenge 3: ⇨		⇨

Devotion 2: The Bible as a Guide

> "...the Bible not only offers some very unique insights into our human nature, but also has the potential to open our minds to the kind of guidance and purpose in life that many of us so passionately seek."
>
> *Read the biblical passages and answer the questions.

2 Timothy 3:16-17   In Context | *Paul, the apostle, writes a young preacher, Timothy, as a mentor.*

Study Reflections	Responses
1. What are four ways in which Scripture can be useful or profitable?	
2. What explanation is given for why these four beneficial uses of Scripture are important?	
3. How can being poorly or inadequately equipped to perform an important job be dangerous?	

Challenge Questions	Responses
4. How can being poorly equipped for good works negatively affect a person or community of people?	
5. What do you think Paul was trying to stress to Timothy by writing this point, in particular?	

(2 Peter 1:20-21)   In Context | *The apostle, Peter, writes a letter reminding Christians of their spiritual duties.*

Study Reflections	Responses
6. What was the first focus Peter highlighted relating to Scriptural prophecy?	
7. From what or where did the words of Scriptural prophecy not originate?	

Study Reflections *(cont.)*	Responses
8. What two spiritual Beings are mentioned as having major roles in guiding men to Scriptural prophecy?	

Challenge Questions	Responses
Read the quote to the right. Then answer the question below.	Quote: *"The Bible is a unique book. It is one of the oldest books in the world, and yet it is still the world's best seller. It is a product of the ancient Eastern world, but it has molded the modern Western world. Tyrants have burned the Bible, and believers revere it. It is the most quoted, the most published, the most translated, and the most influential book in the history of mankind.[1]"*
9. What might be some reasons behind why the Bible continues to hold so much universal appeal, attractiveness, and be so widely used even today?	

Challenge Questions *(cont.)*	Responses
Read the passages to the right. Then answer the question below.	<u>Passages:</u> *"Your word is a lamp unto my feet, and a light unto my path." (Psalm 119:105)* *"...the commandment of the LORD is pure, enlightening the eyes." (Psalm 19:8)*
10. *These scriptures refer to God's guidance and enlightenment. In what ways or areas of your life are you currently seeking direction and guidance?*	

Last One Standing

IN THE BIBLE BOOK OF REVELATION, JESUS communicates a message to the church in a city called Smyrna where Christians were suffering from unimaginable persecution and poverty at the time. He begins His address by describing Himself as *"The First and the Last"*[2]. But what does this mean exactly? And how is it even significant? Realistically, one could easily wonder what value the phrase might hold as one used to identify Christ. But a thorough investigation of how this seemingly simplistic phrase is used throughout scripture offers some intriguing insights about its relevance and modern-day application, as well.

In an earlier biblical passage written hundreds of years before Christ's message came to the city of Smyrna, a surprisingly similar phrase was used by someone who identified Himself as the Creator. He said, *"I am the first and I am the last, and there is no God besides Me. Who is like Me? Let him proclaim and declare it. . ."*[3] In its context, many people who had been believers of this Higher Power

– to whom was attributed the creation of all things – began to reduce their admiration of Him by displacing their worship onto idols and figures crafted by men. This Creator responded with a line of reasoning that offered little hope to those who put their complete trust in just anything or anyone, a fact passionately stressed by His own account, *"Who has fashioned a god or cast an idol to no profit...for the craftsmen themselves are mere men...I the LORD am the maker of all things, stretching out the heavens by Myself and spreading out the earth all alone."*[4] His point was clear, *how can any material thing being worshipped offer more in life than what an Intelligent Designer can provide?* Evidently, He sought to establish a clear distinction between a singular Creator and the multiplicity of other gods invented by men. Similarly, Jesus wanted the Christians in Smyrna to know that He was the real thing – the first, the last, and the only one of His kind, especially when it came to empowering and guiding others through life.

This fact is validated even more strongly when we explore an event that occurred in Jesus' life where He ascended a mountain with three of His very close followers named Peter, James, and John. One biblical account records the event as follows: *"[Jesus'] garments became radiant and exceedingly white, as no launderer on earth can whiten them. Elijah appeared to them along with Moses; and they were talking with Jesus. Peter said to Jesus, 'Rabbi, it is good for us to be here; let us make three tabernacles, one for You, one for Moses, and one for Elijah.' For he did not know what to answer; for they became terrified."*[5] The two men who appeared before Jesus and His three followers were both renowned and highly regarded historical religious figures, especially in the Jewish faith – of which these men were a part. They knew Elijah as a great prophet who showed many wonderful proofs of the Creator's existence and power. Moses was also a familiar household name who, with the Lord's guidance, led the Jewish people from bondage and slavery to help establish a strong and mighty nation. So, it's no surprise that Peter would make the request that he did to establish three tabernacles (or places of worship) for these two historical religious leaders, along with Jesus.

One of the many purposes of the tabernacle was to honor and pay homage to God. Therefore, Peter's request to create three different tabernacles for three different people would seem to show a respectful reverence toward these individuals and what they had accomplished. In fact, many would probably view Peter's request as a very considerate statement toward all of the great religious leaders who were present – with the intent not to offend or belittle any of the contributions made to their own spiritual communities. What's interesting, though, is that his request was made out of fear; and he really had no clue what to say, at all. For what happened directly after his request establishes the premise for a key lesson we should all take away from this event. So the Bible reads, *"Then a cloud formed, overshadowing them, and a voice came out of the cloud, 'This is My beloved Son, listen to Him!' All at once they looked around and saw no one with them anymore, except Jesus alone."*[6] Why was Jesus the last one standing? Surely, He was not the only one who did great things; nor was He the only person to ever promote spiritual devotion and inspire others to be better humans. But according to this scripture, *Christ held a very special and unique role among other religious figures from the perspective of the One who encouraged attention to be given to Him above all others.*

Last One Standing

Devotion 3: In the Mind of God

> "... how can any material thing being worshipped offer more in life than what an Intelligent Designer can provide?"

*Read the passages, complete the activities and answer each question.

Reflection: *List 3 characteristics you would use to describe the nature of God.*		
Characteristic 1:	Characteristic 2:	Characteristic 3:

Acts 17:16-21   In Context | *Paul waits in the city of Athens for two of his companions in another city to meet him.*

1. *What did Paul notice about the city of Athens, and what did he do about it?*

2. *How did the philosophers respond to the things Paul was saying, and what did they do?*

Acts 17:22-29

Reflection: *List 3 characteristics Paul used to describe the nature of God.*		
Characteristic 1:	Characteristic 2:	Characteristic 3:

3. *WHY DO YOU THINK THERE ARE SO MANY MISCONCEPTIONS ABOUT WHO GOD IS AND HOW HE OPERATES?*

Devotion 4: Uniquely Focused

> "... Christ held a very special and unique role among other religious figures from the perspective of the One who encouraged attention to be given to Him above all others."

*Brainstorm a list of famous or well-known religious/spiritual leaders – other than Jesus – from the past and present of any world religion or denomination.

Religious Leaders List	
1.	7.
2.	8.
3.	9.
4.	10.
5.	11.
6.	12.

From this list, select 2 leaders that stand out as particularly significant to you; and write their names in the blanks below:

(A) _____   (B) _____

Mark 9:2-8

In Context: Three of Jesus' apostles travel with Him atop a mountain and witness a special event.

Study Reflections	Responses
1. How did God respond to Peter's suggestion of making three tabernacles (places of worship) for three different religious leaders?	

Challenge Questions	Responses
2. What point does it seem like God was making by His response?	
3. Based on the focus and tone of this passage, how do you think God would have responded if the suggestion was made to create a place of worship for Jesus along with any of the other spiritual/religious leaders mentioned on the previous page?	

Powerless Philosophies

NEVER SETTLING FOR ANYTHING LESS THAN THE REAL thing can always come with great benefits and advantages. But looks can be deceiving; and it is not, at all, uncommon for something to appear like a quality product when, in reality, it lacks those necessary elements to actually perform its designated task effectively. This same concept can be applied to most any area of our lives, but especially when it involves our spiritual nature. Practicing religion, for example, is seen by many people as a means to help us understand and promote universal qualities like peace, fairness, justice, and service toward others. It's also viewed as a safety net to assist us in providing restraints for overindulging in things that can be destructive to self and detrimental to others. But what happens if the ways we've learned to behave, think, and talk from our religion lacks substance in actually helping us to achieve these ends? How, you might ask? Well, this exact point was addressed in a biblical passage by a man who converted to Christianity after brutally persecuting Christians earlier in his life. His name was Paul, and after his conversion he frequently sent letters to encourage the church throughout as many geographic regions as possible. One letter to Christians in a city called Colossae included a very strong emphasis on the special characteristics and unmatched uniqueness of Jesus Christ. Unfortunately, a good number of Christians there were following religious practices and commands based more on customs and traditions put in place by men rather than Jesus. Paul, in his letter to the Colossians, summarized there mistake in this way: *"These are matters which have, to be sure, the appearance of wisdom in self-made religion and self-abasement and severe treatment of the body, but are of no value against fleshly indulgence."*[7] Wow! What a powerful conclusion! This kind of revolutionary statement warrants so much more examination and reflection. Essentially, he told these Christians *they were doing things that, at least, looked like and appeared to be religious. But for all of their efforts, nothing they did was really able to help prevent them from overindulging in their flesh.* By the "flesh," Paul was referring to those things that can eventually destroy both our body and spirit. He even made reference to a few activities of the flesh in a letter written to Christians of the city Galatia: *"Now the deeds of the flesh are evident, which are: immorality, impurity, sensuality, sorcery, enmities, strife, jealousy, outbursts of anger, disputes, dissensions, factions, envying, drunkenness, carousing and things like these..."*[8] When any of these examples he identified (or similar activities) reach their most devastating height, they can utterly destroy individuals, families, and communities in a number of different ways. How defeating it would be, then, to spend, time, effort, and energy into practices that are supposed to help correct these behaviors but are powerless to do so. Placing our complete trust only in people, who are flawed and prone to error, will cause this. That is not to say that no one can be trusted or followed, but there should be parameters and conditions for who we allow to lead us spiritually. Paul highlighted the most important condition in his first letter to the Corinthian Christians: *"Be imitators of me, just as I also am of*

[Jesus] Christ."[9] This is why having the real thing is so important. Jesus' unique role and relationship with the Creator gives him a revolutionary perspective of how to bring about true, consistent, and long-lasting change; but philosophies that find their root in anyone or anything else fundamentally lack the substance to produce these kinds of quality results. Referring to the Creator as his Father, Jesus describes their closeness in this way: *"I am the way, and the truth, and the life; no one comes to the Father but through me."*[10] Who else can claim this kind of rare intimacy with the Creator? Jesus holds all the keys and can guide us in not only reversing destructive trends, but also helping us understand the reasoning behind their occurrences so that we can avoid them in the future and progress in powerful and mature spiritual directions.

Devotion 5: Rescue Option

> "... they were doing things that, at least, looked like and appeared to be religious. But for all of their efforts, nothing they did was really able to help prevent them from overindulging in their flesh."

*Read the passages and complete the activities below.

Galatians 5:19-21	In Context	Paul offers examples of activities that can be spiritually destructive and unhealthy.

1. List three of the fleshly deeds or activities Paul mentioned in his letter to the Galatians with which you or someone you know has personally had to wrestle.

2. In the sections that follow, describe specific ways in which each of the deeds you selected above can be destructive or unhealthy for individuals, families, and communities.

Fleshly deed 1: _____

Individuals:
Families:
Communities:

Fleshly deed 2: _____

Individuals:
Families:
Communities:

Fleshly deed 3: _____

Individuals:
Families:
Communities:

Romans 7:18-25 | In Context | *Paul writes Christians about the ongoing struggle between our fleshly desire to please self and spiritual desire to please God.*

Just like all of us, Paul experienced a very personal struggle with certain fleshly deeds. He called these fleshly deeds sin; and at its worst point, he described this sin in a way that seemed to control or "take over" his body. Not that he was unable to stop it, but that his will, alone, seemed to lack the strength to overcome it completely. So, he referred to this enslaving effect of sin on himself as producing a body of death.

3. What statement and question was Paul passionately led to ask toward the end of this passage?

Colossians 2:1-3, 8	In Context	Paul writes Christians about the struggles he endured for their encouragement and Christ's uniqueness.

4. What did Paul say was hidden in Christ, and how might this affect overcoming the fleshly deeds that enslave us?

5. What do these passages say about the effectiveness of trying to overcome sin with methods that have no root or foundation in Jesus?

The Cost of Acceptance

FOR MOST OF US, WE KNOW WHEN SOMETHING IS quality and when it's not. So, whenever an opportunity presents itself, it only make sense to reject whatever's lacking in quality and to acquire that which is the most valuable. What, then, would be the reasoning behind purposely choosing something that is less than the best? Or why would anyone avoid getting the absolute best if it were available? These are two very necessary and pertinent questions to ask if Jesus is, in fact, that quality presence for which the whole of humanity yearns. And the fact that we are social creatures, by nature, may have something to do with the answers. *Popularity and peer pressure often greatly influence our actions. Sometimes, they even drive us to reject the things that can benefit us the most.*

As a man who formerly murdered Christians and dismissed any belief that had to do with Jesus, the apostle Paul understood this very well. His experiences led him to passionately articulate some ideas to Christians in the city of Galatia who were allowing others to distort

Christ's message in its purest form: *"I am amazed that you are so quickly deserting [the Creator] who called you by the grace of Christ for a different gospel..."*[11] This "gospel" he wrote of is best explained in his own words: *"...that Christ died for our sins according to the Scriptures, and that He was buried, and that He was raised on the third day according to the Scriptures."*[12] Because the legitimacy of this statement could be understandably scrutinized in its most literal form, it will be explored in more detail throughout the next lesson. But at this juncture it's important to highlight Paul's concern that the church in Galatia was being led astray with a different version of this gospel. In fact, he explained it to be more of a perversion than an actual deviation or change. And as he continued asking them questions, we begin to grasp why they had even allowed this drifting from the truth to occur in the first place. He enquired, *"...am I now seeking the favor of men or of God? Or am I striving to please men? If I were still trying to please men, I would not be a bond-servant of Christ."*[13] Amazingly, these words were written to people centuries ago; yet many of us still face this same dilemma today of either denying or distorting those very things that could bring balance and completeness to our lives at the cost of being socially accepted. Jesus knew this, perhaps, better than any other person. While He was immensely popular during certain years of His public ministry, His fame eventually began to fluctuate as He continued addressing topics and issues that many people really didn't want to hear. One passage explains an instance where an entire crowd of people walked off from His teaching, many of them because He said some things that were difficult to accept and understand. His twelve closest followers, also known as apostles, were present at this event – here's how the latter stages unfolded: *"...Jesus said to the twelve, 'You do not want to go away also, do you?' Simon Peter answered Him, 'Lord, to whom shall we go? You have words of eternal life. We have believed and have come to know that You are the Holy One of God.'"*[14]

Peter's experiences led him to realize that Jesus was an especially rare commodity in mankind's past, present, and future –

like no other person would ever be before, during, and after Him. More than that, he was unwilling to depart from the only person he believed could provide true, sustained, life-altering direction. Even later in life, Peter's passion for who Jesus was and what He could do for others drove him to endure great persecution, hardships, and rejection. Yet, he remained loyal to his conviction of Christ's uniqueness and supremacy over everyone else – including himself. This sentiment is expressed very clearly in a passage where he was arrested and questioned for promoting Jesus through his teaching and assistance of a crippled man. Leaving no room for anyone to doubt his core beliefs, Peter's reply included a discourse about Jesus that ended with these words: *"...there is salvation in no one else; for there is no other name under heaven that has been given among men by which we must be saved."*[15] The finality and absoluteness of such a statement warrants a special consideration of Christ's life, attitude, way of thinking, and interaction with others – a man who is still affecting powerful change in the world today, even after his physical departure from it thousands of years ago. What reasoning can be offered to explain such an intriguing phenomenon? There simply has never been, nor will there ever be, any one like Him – the first…the last…the only…real thing!

The Cost of Acceptance

Devotion 6: Seeking Approval

> *"Popularity and peer pressure often greatly influence our actions. Sometimes, they even drive us to reject the things that can benefit us the most."*

* Read the biblical passage, and answer the questions below.

John 12:42-43 — In Context: *After performing miraculous signs, many began to believe in Jesus' claim to divinity; but they were unwilling to admit it openly.*

Study Reflections	Responses
1. What caused the rulers who believed in Jesus to avoid confessing Him?	
2. Whose approval were these rulers seeking?	
3. In what ways can seeking the approval of other people become unhealthy and destructive?	

Challenge Questions	Responses
4. What short term challenges might we sometimes encounter by seeking God's approval over other's approval?	
Read the passage to the right. Then answer the question below.	Passage: "Jesus said, 'Truly I say to you, there is no one who has left house or brothers or sisters or mother or father or children or farms, for My sake and for the gospel's sake, but that he will receive a hundred times as much now in the present age, houses and brothers and sisters and mothers and children and farms, along with persecutions; and in the age to come, eternal life.'" (Mark 10:29-30)
5. According to this passage, what long term benefits are associated with seeking God's approval over the approval of everyone else?	

SECTION TWO

Destined For Each Other

Directions of Fulfillment

Directions of Fulfillment

MY WEDDING WAS IN A COUPLE OF MONTHS, AND I can remember sitting next to the window in my old room praying about the woman I was going to marry. Almost a year and a half earlier – days after I had met her for the first time – I recall thinking how magnificently unreal it was to meet someone who felt so compatible with me. But previous experiences taught me to move carefully and cautiously, despite how well our first few interactions went. Some would even view our first meeting and the events that occurred throughout our courtship as pure lucky chance, but I know better. My fiancée's very close friend had been married to an active duty military man at the time, and they had lived throughout the country in many different cities for most of their marriage. But it wasn't until they moved to my hometown that the woman who would eventually become my wife was actually able to pay her friend a visit. Coincidentally, the couple happened to be friends of my family; so when a chance encounter occurred with this beautiful woman from out of town who was meeting her friend, sparks flew between us! The chemistry was obvious. Our conversations lasted for hours, and neither of us could spend enough time together. Only, she lived over a thousand miles away; and I wasn't sure if I could really know a person from that distance, although, I was willing to try. If only there was a way for us to be closer. As it turned out, a few weeks after meeting her I learned that almost an entire year of my military training would be in a city only a few hours from her hometown. Of all the places it could be, how conveniently accommodating! With frequent visits whenever military leave permitted, our bond and fondness for one another grew. The proposal was inevitable. She was the woman I wanted and needed; and I was the man for whom she longed. Was it destiny? Nothing in my experience with her had led me to believe otherwise. So months before the wedding, as I was praying next to my window, I figured that amazing things would continue to happen if this relationship was truly meant to be – and they did!

Focusing all of my attention and finances on the basics like securing a job, housing, food, and transportation caused me to overlook a few other details. I realized this when I finally got a moment to sit down and create a list of all the things I needed to do before the wedding. Furniture was one of many items on that list. The apartment we would move into was completely bare; but like many engaged couples, so were our wallets! While contemplating what to do about this, my fiancée gave me a call with some wonderful news. Her uncle had just recently gotten married and was thinking about selling an entire house full of extra furniture he had. Instead, he decided to give it to us – free of charge – everything! After the initial shock, we set to the task of finding a way to transport all of our newly acquired furnishings. But the furniture was a whopping seventeen hour drive from where it needed to go, and it would require way more than a simple pick-up truck to transport it all. What's more, renting the size of moving truck we needed involved finding someone who had a special driver's license; and the cost of going one way – as opposed to round trip – at that distance was much too ridiculous to even contemplate. Ironically, a family friend from my hometown gave me a call a few days later. He happened to be a professional truck driver and had learned I was getting married in the same city he would be traveling through shortly after our wedding. As a gift, he offered to transport anything we needed and even pay for all moving truck expenses – down to the last penny! That situation couldn't have worked out more perfectly! And that's not even skimming the surface of how so many things worked out so smoothly during our courtship, wedding, and even after it. In the past I had been in love before and even contemplated marriage, but events always seemed to unfold that would dissolve those relationships before they reached maturity. This time was different, though. The exact opposite happened. Everything, seemingly, fell into place in the right way and at the right time. It was as if we were destined for each other – meant to be together; and even though life wasn't perfect – as it never is – there was still something right within my spirit and complete within the world around me from simply being in a relationship that brought such wholeness to my existence.

Some call it destiny; others call it fate. But whatever we choose to name it is of no consequence. We all know what it means – the idea that certain events will happen or take place, regardless of any efforts made to prevent them. And whether you believe in this concept or not, it's a topic that we're forced to explore when investigating the way in which Jesus describes Himself to the church in Smyrna long ago: *"[The One]...who was dead and has come to life."*[1] But before looking into how this topic relates to the concept of destiny, it's necessary to address the validity of the statement, itself. Has anyone who ever died physically, for example, truly been able to return to the realm of the living? Many would dismiss the very notion as completely ridiculous without even seeing the need to explore it any further; and most attempts to understand the possibility of such an event taking place would eventually steer into the area of the supernatural where discussion of a Divine Being might soon follow. Words from a former atheist articulates this sentiment very appropriately: *"The mere idea of an all-powerful, all-knowing, all-loving Creator of the universe seemed so absurd to me that it wasn't even worth my time to check out."*[2] So then, how does a person with such strong convictions as these ultimately arrive at the following place of curiosity: *"...I decided to use my journalism and legal training to systematically investigate whether there was credibility to any religion – especially Christianity. This launched me into what turned out to be a nearly two-year spiritual quest."*[3] While it's fascinating that someone who was unwilling to examine the potential of a Supreme Being would eventually spend so much time researching religion, equally intriguing are the factors that could influence such a broad change of heart. For this particular person, those factors included changes he noticed in his wife's values and behavior when she decided to become a follower of Jesus, in conjunction with a lack of fulfillment and satisfaction in his own life. He described it in this way, *"I had a lot of anger inside of me. If you had asked me back then why I was so mad, I don't think I could have explained it. But looking back, I can see that I was always after the perfect high and the ultimate experience of pleasure. But in the end, everything would end in bitter disappointment."*[4]

In a similar comment, a very wealthy and powerful king of the Israelite nation who lived long ago had also vigorously searched for self-fulfillment by exerting an astronomical amount of effort and resources into anything he thought might bring him pleasure. But when all was said and done, he came to discover a very clear reality that he communicated with the following words:

I explored in my mind how to stimulate my body with wine...I built houses for myself...I made gardens and parks for myself...I made ponds of water for myself with which to irrigate a forest of growing trees...I bought male and female slaves...Also, I collected for myself silver and gold and the treasure of kings and provinces. I provided for myself male and female singers and the pleasures of men – many concubines. Then I became great and increased more than all who preceded me in Jerusalem...All that my eyes desired I did not refuse them. I did not withhold my heart from any pleasure...Thus I considered all my activities which my hand had done and the labor which I had exerted, and behold all was vanity and striving after the wind and there was no profit under the sun.[5]

How could a man with all of these things say that there was no profit in any of them? The very thought of it can be completely baffling to some! But one of the most insightful passages in scripture can open our eyes to how and why he reached this conclusion: *"I know, O LORD, that a man's way is not in himself, nor is it in man who walks to direct his steps."*[6] Consider these words very carefully. They say, in essence, that *humans lack the full capacity within themselves to be their own guide throughout life. And when we do attempt to fulfill this guiding role ourselves; we begin to notice a void in our lives that can neither be completely filled by other humans, nor by anything else that humans can create.* Of course, some may completely reject this statement, altogether. But time and experience may prove otherwise, and many of us have come to learn that demonstrations can often be much more effective than explanations. By this, I mean that there are some things we can discover from our experiences in life that we simply won't be able to grasp with our intellect alone. And just like the gentleman who had been an atheist with no desire to explore a Higher Power, his experiences led him to a different place he'd never imagined being. That is not to discourage us from rendering as important those necessary intellectual proofs required to establish a belief in something, only to highlight the influence our experiences have on the mental, emotional, and spiritual parts of our being, as well. People will always have very calculated experiences that lead them to destinations of curiosity about their purpose and direction. Why? Because this is where the natural void we have will always take us. It may be sooner rather than later. It could occur earlier in life or on a person's death bed. It might not even come until after we've exhausted all other useless attempts to achieve long-term satisfaction. But the void will always remain until we decide to fill it properly. And when our experiences do lead us to that point in time, we begin to wonder who or what can fill this void we have; and how. Perhaps, the best answer to that question involves a thorough exploration of every possible resource relating to the topic. And because of its theme, unique content, and historical design; the Bible should, undoubtedly, be considered as a primary source in this quest. In fact, note the words of one skeptic's take on some of its contents: *"While I wasn't prepared to accept these writings as divinely inspired, I was forced to evaluate them for what they undeniably are: A set of ancient historical documents. And I knew that just as Historians investigate the reliability of such writers as Josephus and Tacitus, they can also use the same techniques to assess the trustworthiness of the Gospels and the rest of the New Testament accounts."*[7]

As these accounts are constantly scrutinized and critiqued for their accuracy, their credibility has not only been established, but maintained time and again. A plethora of literature has been written on this topic. And for those interested in a more intensive study of the

Bible, its development, and divine authority; there's a recommended list of literature to explore in a latter section of this volume. Our focus here, however, lies in what these writings say about filling the void in our lives and understanding our purpose.

Directions of Fulfillment

Devotion 7: Navigation Necessities

". . . humans lack the full capacity within themselves to be their own guide throughout life. And when we do attempt to fulfill this guiding role ourselves; we begin to notice a void in our lives that can neither be completely filled by other humans, nor by anything else that humans can create."

*Read the passages, and answer the questions.

Proverbs 3:5-8 | In Context | *A prosperous king, Solomon, offers words of wisdom about life, in general*

Study Reflections	Responses
1. What two things did Solomon mention that should not be done?	
2. What three things did Solomon encourage to be done?	
3. What benefits did Solomon suggest would occur from following the advice he offers?	

Challenge Questions	Responses
Read the passage to the right, and answer the question below.	<u>Passage</u>: *"'For my thoughts are not your thoughts, nor are your ways My ways,' declares the Lord. 'For as the heavens are higher than the earth, so are My ways higher than your ways and My thoughts than your thoughts.'"* (Isaiah 55:8-9)
4. Based on the previous passage, circle the characteristics on the right that you would assign to God?	Rookie Master Amateur Professional Novice Veteran
5. How can trusting in someone with the characteristics you circled be beneficial in life and how can trusting in ourselves be detrimental at times?	

Proverbs 14:12; 16:2, 25; 21:2

6. What do these passages say about the faultiness of each person developing his or her own ethical standard or moral compass in life?

Proverbs 30:5

7. What does this passage say God is for all people who put their trust in Him?

8. What kind of protection would anyone seek (or could anyone benefit from) while living in a world like ours?

Ecclesiastes 12:13

9. This writer, who sought fulfillment in many different worldly pleasures, was ultimately disappointed and left empty in his search. But what conclusion or summary did he eventually reach in this passage about being fulfilled?

What's the Plan, Here?

IN A VERY SPECIAL LETTER TO CHRISTIANS FROM THE city of Ephesus, the apostle Paul brought to light a few of the most foundational principles about the Creator – who he called, God – and that Creator's purpose for humanity. Written with divine guidance, this letter is one of the books in the Bible; and the introduction includes these words: *"[God] chose us in Him before the foundation of the world, that we would be holy and blameless before Him. In love He predestined us to adoption as sons through Jesus Christ to Himself, according to the kind intention of His will."*[8] The crystal clear emphasis to these Christians could never be mistaken. Simply put, God had a plan for humanity before the world – or anything in it – was ever created. This plan was not to be a passive and distant observer of the human experience. Rather, it involved a proactive participation on His part for all people, but especially toward those who would be willing to amend their lifestyles to coincide with His will. And for those people, in particular, He would establish a very special relationship, like a loving parent does with a child. Most importantly, though, that closeness with the Creator could only come through and because of Jesus Christ. Paul explains how this is when he writes, *"In [Jesus] we have redemption through His blood, the forgiveness of our trespasses, according to the riches of His grace."*[9] The Christians who were written here already understood that deviating from the Creator's will is known as sin. They also knew that no human – save one – ever had the fortitude and endurance to live in complete submission to the Creator's will without falling short of it. That person was Jesus, and His very passionate internal drive to please the Creator at all costs offers many clues into how He was even able to achieve this sinless existence. What's most significant, however – not only for the Christians in Ephesus, but for any person in any time – is that sin creates a separation from God for all who participate in it. One passage concludes, *"...your iniquities have made a separation between you and your God, and your sins have hidden His face from you so that He does not hear."*[10] This separation severs the opportunity for intimacy with the Creator, which also prevents the void we all have from being filled. Equally important is the fact that sin automatically earns and eventually brings about both a physical and spiritual death to everyone who has it. *But God, understanding the potential for human frailty and error, designed a plan for humanity by which intimacy with Him could be restored and sins could be completely eliminated as if they never even occurred.* This plan, known as the gospel or "good news", required Jesus – as the only sinless being – to suffer a cruel and criminal death on behalf of humanity so that we could graciously receive those privileges we are not able to earn ourselves: intimacy with the Creator and forgiveness of our sins. Paul summarizes it best when he writes these words to Christians in the ancient city of Corinth, *"Now I make known to you, brethren, the gospel which I preached to you, which also you received, in which also you stand, by which also you are saved, if you hold fast the word which I preached to you, unless you believed in vain. For I delivered to you as of first importance what I also received, that Christ died for our sins according to the Scriptures, and that He was buried, and that He was raised on the third day according to the Scriptures…"*[11]

Devotion 8: Researching Renewal

> "... God, understanding the potential for human frailty and error, designed a plan for humanity by which intimacy with Him could be restored and sins could be completely eliminated as if they never even occurred."

*Read the passages and complete the activities.

Acts 2:22-24 **In Context** *The Apostle, Peter, teaches a large diverse crowd of people gathered in the city of Jerusalem.*

Briefly summarize each of the following verses from Peter's Sermon.

Summaries		
Acts 2:22	Acts 2:23	Acts 2:24

What's the Plan, Here

For each passage, write the correct letter that belongs with it from the categories list below.

Context	Passages	Categories
A prophecy foretelling events in Christ's life	1. ____ Isaiah 53:3-10	A. Miracles, wonders & signs B. Crucifixion & plan C. Resurrection
Jesus visits his hometown	2. ____ Matthew 13:53-58	
Jesus has a conversation with his disciples	3. ____ Luke 9:18-22	
Jesus is on trial before different leaders	4. ____ Luke 23:2-8	
Events taking place after Christ's trial	5. ____ Luke 24:1-12	
A man converses with Jesus by night	6. ____ John 3:1-2	
One man teaches another about Jesus	7. ____ Acts 8:26-35	
The apostle Paul teaches Christians	8. ____ 1 Corinthians 15:50-58	
Paul explains a concept to Christians	9. ____ Ephesians 1:5-7	

Matthew 2:19-23 — In Context | *God guides Jesus' earthly father, Joseph*

10. *In what regions and city did Joseph and his family eventually settle?*

Devotion 9: Specialized Selections

> "... God, understanding the potential for human frailty and error, designed a plan for humanity by which intimacy with Him could be restored and sins could be completely eliminated as if they never even occurred."

*Read the passages and answer the questions below.

Psalm 16:8-11   **In Context** | *The king of Israel, David, writes about the Lord's goodness.*

Study Reflections	Responses
1. What did David say about what the Lord would show or make known to him?	
2. What did David say could be found in the Lord's presence?	
3. What did David mention concerning the Lord's right hand?	

Challenge Questions	Responses
4. How could the things David mentioned benefit those who look to the Lord for guidance?	
5. Why might so many people think that following the Lord produces the exact opposite of the things David mentioned?	

Acts 2:25-32   In Context | *Peter, the apostle, teaches others about a prophecy of Jesus.*

6. According to verses 29-31, what did Peter say was the broader prophetic meaning of the Psalm David wrote?

What's the Plan, Here

Psalm 89:3-4	In Context	A covenant the Lord had made concerning the descendant of king David is foretold.

7. In which verse of Acts 2:25-32 did Peter mention this same prophecy?

8. In Acts 2:32, Peter said he and others were witnesses of Jesus resurrected. Read Acts 1:1-3, and answer the following questions:

   a. Jesus showed himself alive to his apostles for how many days after his suffering?

   b. What did Jesus speak to the apostles about after he suffered?

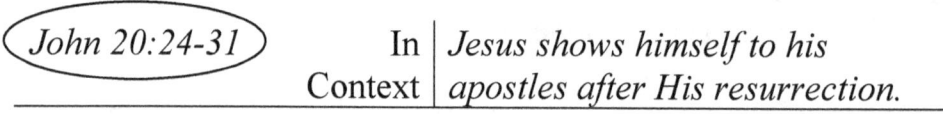

John 20:24-31	In Context	Jesus shows himself to his apostles after His resurrection.

9. What two reasons are given for why the miraculous signs Jesus performed were written?

Jesus knew that he wouldn't always be around in a physical sense to perform miraculous signs as proof of His divine nature. But while he was on earth in human form, He passed on His miraculous powers to His apostles.

Read Matthew 10:1-4. Then, write the names of the original twelve apostles Jesus selected?

Original Apostles List	
1.	7.
2.	8.
3.	9.
4.	10.
5.	11.
6.	12.

What's the Plan, Here

Acts 1:15-26 — In Context | Another apostle is selected in place of Judas, who betrayed Christ.

10. What was the name of the apostle who replaced Judas?

Acts 22:1-21 — In Context | Paul explains and defends his Christian conversion to a doubtful crowd.

Find the answer to each question, and list the verse where you found it.

11. What did Paul do to men and women who followed the "way" of Jesus?	
Answer:	vs.

12. What did Ananias instruct Paul to do?	
Answer:	vs.

13. To whom would Paul become a witness; and what would he witness about?	
Answer:	vs.

14. To whom did the Lord say He would send Paul?	
Answer:	vs.

Rare Treasure of Destiny

Romans 1:1-5 — In Context | *Paul explains the gospel and his apostolic mission.*

15. Verse 5 shows that Paul's mission as an apostle was specifically directed toward what group of people?

1 Corinthians 15:8-11 — In Context | *Paul shares how his apostleship happened in a rare way and at a unique time.*

16. How does Paul describe the way Jesus appeared to him as the last apostle?

17. How does Paul compare himself to the other apostles; and why?

As a very rare and specially selected group of individuals, the apostles were given authority and powers by Jesus that other humans never

What's the Plan, Here

possessed. These included empowering others with miraculous abilities to perform signs and wonders, also.

(Acts 8:4-24)	In Context	*The early church is greatly persecuted and scatters to many different places, as a result.*

18. What reason does the text give for why the people followed Simon?

19. What did Simon offer the apostles and why?

20. How did the apostles respond to Simon?

21. What discovery did Simon make in verse 18 of this chapter?

22. Read Acts 6:1-6. What conclusion can be drawn from the passage about the origin of Philip's miraculous powers?

Just like Jesus performed signs as proof of His message being divine, miracles like the ones Philip performed occurred during the time of the early church to help validate the trustworthiness of its message, as well.

Mark 16:14-20

23. How was the word the apostles preached confirmed?

While neither Jesus nor the apostles He selected exist today in human form, the Bible does familiarize us with how God's message is validated and confirmed in this day and age. Devotions 11 and 12 briefly explore this topic.

What's the Plan, Here

Devotion 10: Fortunes of Fascination

> "... God, understanding the potential for human frailty and error, designed a plan for humanity by which intimacy with Him could be restored and sins could be completely eliminated as if they never even occurred."

*Read the passages, and complete the activities.

| Acts 1:1-11 | In Context | Luke, the physician, records a detailed account of events that occurred shortly before Jesus ascends to heaven in human form. |

*Select the correct word for each blank from the Word Bank on the next page.

The (1) _____ that Jesus selected were commanded not to leave the city of (2) _____, but to wait for what the Father (3) _____ them, which included being (4) _____ with the (5) _____ _____. Jesus also told them that they would receive (6) _____ when the Holy Spirit came upon them and that they would be witnesses in Jerusalem, Judea, Samaria, and in all parts of the (7) _____. After this,

Jesus was lifted up on a cloud out of their sight while two men in (8) _____ told the apostles – men of (9) _____ – that Jesus would come back in the same way they watched him go into (10) _____.

Word Bank:

Apostles	loving God	Charge	followed	promised
Bethlehem	Nazareth	courage	grasp	rulers
Galilee	new law	directed	heaven	sight
Holy Spirit	Pharisees	earth	let	villages
Jerusalem	baptized	faith	power	white

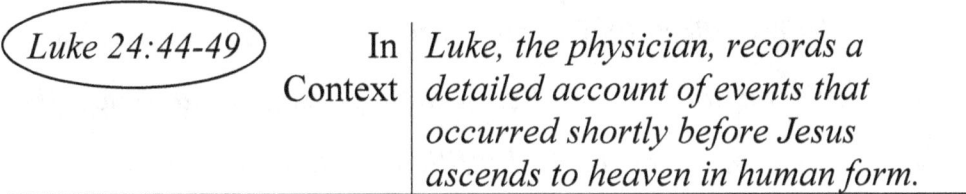

In Context | *Luke, the physician, records a detailed account of events that occurred shortly before Jesus ascends to heaven in human form.*

1. What did Jesus say must be fulfilled?

2. What did Jesus say was written about the Christ?

What's the Plan, Here

Use the passage from Luke 24:44-49 to answer the two questions below.

Prophecy	Question: *What did Jesus say he was going to send (v.49)?*	Question: *In what nations was repentance for the forgiveness of sins supposed to be preached or proclaimed, and in what city was this to begin? (v.47)?*
	Answer:	Answer:
Fulfilled	(A)	

The passages below offer clues to the fulfillment of the prophecies in the "Prophecy" section above. Read each passage and place the letters beside them in the correct "Fulfilled" column above. The first one has been done for you.

Passages

(A) *Acts 2:1-4*   (B) *Acts 2:5*   (C) *Acts 2:6-8*

(D) *Acts 2:9-10*   (E) *Acts 2:11-13*   (F) *Acts 2:33*

Acts 2:14-21   In Context | *Peter, the apostle, explains the miraculous events occurring on the Day of Pentecost as the fulfillment of a prophecy.*

3. *What prophet did Peter refer to as making this prophecy?*

4. *What did God say He would pour in verses 17 and 18?*

5. *What did God say He would do in verse 19?*

Luke 24:44-49   In Context | *Luke, the physician, records a detailed account of events that occurred shortly before Jesus ascends to heaven in human form.*

6. *Who did God make to be both Lord and Christ?*

7. *This passage indicates that Peter was teaching to people who had actively participated in what?*

Exhibit E - Experience

WHILE THE CREATOR'S PLAN FOR HUMANITY IS understood and accepted by many people, a few obvious concerns naturally arise for others, as a belief in events that clearly lie outside of the physical realm is required. Believing in the physical death and resurrection of a person is simply too difficult a concept to fathom for some. To that point, one theologian has asked the following questions: *"...is it possible that the portrait of the divine Son of God is an exaggeration, at best, or a complete fabrication, at worst, of the original Jesus? Could the one whom Christians worship be merely a mythological creation or is he real?"*[12] If the Creator's plan is ever to be proven accurate, the heart and soul of any answer to these questions must never avoid a doubter's perspective. The same theologian explains, *"...skeptics begin by affirming that there are no miracles, nothing supernatural in this world. Therefore, the story of Jesus cannot be true."*[13] With these kinds of assumptions, many begin to wonder if God's plan for humanity is nothing more than a crazed conspiracy or human hoax. Our natural curiosity and capacity for intellectual reasoning, however, should steer us toward areas such as history or science for further proof.

Historically speaking, many details of Jesus' life and death can be gathered and investigated by using systematic methods of inquiry. But just like with any other ancient historical event or person, there may always be certain details we simply cannot assess indefinitely. So, while history can be extremely helpful in many ways, it still has certain limitations. Turning to science can also assist us with providing logical explanations for a great number of extraordinary events. But, unfortunately, there are even limitations in this field of study. Notice the conclusion a passionate physical science student reached after experiencing repeated disappointment from his professor's inability to answer questions about the origin of life:

I asked this professor what the process was by which the original life--the original living cells upon the earth--came into existence. How did the structure or generation of DNA occur? Once again, this man said, "Young man, that is not a question that falls within the realm of science." In today's world we understand more about biochemical processes, but we cannot answer how in the environment of the primitive earth these processes came into operation. I guess what was happening to me was the same thing that Lord Kelvin, a very famous British scientist, described in his writings when he made the statement, "If you study science deep enough and long enough it will force you to believe in God." That is what happened to me. I began to realize that science had its limitations--that science, in fact, strongly pointed to other explanations than natural ones to certain questions.[14]

How, then, can anyone determine the legitimacy of God's plan for humanity if so many sources we look to as reliable are limited in their ability to completely reassure us of its accuracy? One would assume that this is exactly the kind of question an all-powerful and all-knowing Creator would anticipate from humans. That is precisely why He *does* provide ways for us to be assured – not only of His presence, but also of His involvement in our lives. But similar to the conclusion reached by the science student; the Creator operates in ways that do include, but are not limited to, the natural and physical world. This is not at all unreasonable when considering the essence of a Divine Being who possesses both infinite and invisible qualities. Take the concept of faith, for example. Some view it as a touchy-feely, superstitious idea for ignorant people. The Bible, however, paints a dramatically different picture. One passage defines it very clearly, *"Now faith is the assurance of things hoped for, the conviction of things not seen."*[15] How is it really possible, though, to be assured and convicted of what we cannot actually see? Because *God, with an intimate knowledge of who we are, often seeks to convict us of who He is through the experiences we have.* History, science, or any other area of study can greatly aid our intellectual understanding and belief in God or Jesus, but these means alone were never intended to sustain our convictions entirely. True faith is established by practice and experiencing the Creator's involvement throughout life in very intimate ways. In fact, it actually resembles a process quite similar to the scientific method:

Exhibit E - Experience

1. *We begin by asking questions:* Does God exist? Was Jesus real? Is God's plan of salvation for humanity legitimate?

2. *A hypothesis is then formulated:* If I devote myself to following God's teachings in the Bible like others have, my life's purpose and direction will be made clearer, I will experience a more satisfying existence, and I'll open myself up to receiving the Creator's deliverance and guidance through difficult circumstances.

3. Upon testing the hypothesis, *we analyze our findings and draw reasonable conclusions:* Did God deliver on his promises? Did I deliver on mine? Did I attempt to conduct my experiment fairly, or was I purposely biased?

4. Lastly, *we communicate our results to others* and begin the process all over again; perhaps with different questions or new insights to previous enquiries.

Of course, learning the Creator's will begins not only with a desire to accept and follow it, but also with a confidence that He is able to provide all that He actually promises. A Biblical passage written to Hebrew Christians emphasizes this, *"...without faith, it is impossible to please [God], for he who comes to God must believe that He [exists] and that He is a rewarder of those who seek Him."*[16]

For a true follower of Jesus, His death, burial, and resurrection are much more than a story to be proven. They are models by which to mimic our lifestyles; and they signify the very plan predestined for humanity by the Creator. A plan designed to free us from the bondage of sin and self-centeredness, to help us know God closely, and to show us life's true fulfillment. The apostle Paul described it most appropriately in this way:

> *...do you not know that all of us who have been baptized into Christ Jesus have been baptized into his death? Therefore we have been buried with Him through baptism into death, so that as Christ was raised from the dead through the glory of the Father, so we too might walk in newness of life...knowing this,*

that our old self was crucified with Him, in order that our body of sin might be done away with, so that we would no longer be slaves to sin...Therefore, do not let sin reign in your mortal body so that you obey its lusts, and do not go on presenting the members of your body to sin as instruments of unrighteousness; but present yourselves to God as those alive from the dead, and your members as instruments of righteousness to God.[17]

Devotion 11: Answering the Call

> *"For a true follower of Jesus, His death, burial, and resurrection is much more than a story to be proven. It is a model by which to mimic one's lifestyle . . ."*

*Use the passages to answer the questions and complete the activities.

Acts 2:37-39	In Context	People who had been instrumental in the crucifixion of Jesus realize their error.

Study Reflections	Responses
1. What question was Peter and the rest of the apostles asked?	
2. Peter responded to the question by telling the crowd to do what two things?	
3. For what reason or purpose did Peter give for telling the crowd to do these things?	

Exhibit E - Experience

Study Reflections *(cont.)*	Responses
4. What did Peter tell the people they would receive upon doing these things?	
5. To whom was this promise that Peter talked about available?	

While Christians today don't have the miraculous measure of the Holy Spirit that Jesus and His apostles possessed, the promised gift of the Holy Spirit that Peter spoke of still powerfully works in each Christian today helping to ensure God's trustworthiness and reliability in His followers' lives.

1 Corinthians 2:7-11	In Context	*Paul informs Christians in the city of Corinth about the Spirit's role.*

Paul explains that no living person is able to fathom or even perceive all the wonderful things God has prepared for humanity. But with the Spirit – and only with the Spirit, God reveals all the benefits and advantages available to humanity for those who love and follow Him.

6. *Based on 1 Corinthians 2:7-11, what role does the Spirit play in helping to establish faith?*

7. *According to Peter's teaching in Acts 2:37-39, under what condition is the Holy Spirit received?*

8. *Read Ephesians 1:13-14. What caused these Christians to be sealed with the Holy Spirit of promise?*

1 Corinthians 2:12-14	In Context	*Paul explains how those without the Spirit do not understand the benefits that come along with having it and consider them to be foolish*

9. *What reason does Paul offer for people not being able to know or understand the things that come from the Spirit?*

Paul realized that every single event occurring in our lives can lead us to true fulfillment and a deeper understanding of our designated purpose and existence. But without the Spirit's guidance, we do not have the full capacity within ourselves to grasp, interpret, or even see how these events are unfolding from a spiritual perspective because it requires a possession of the Holy Spirit, which can only come through obedience of the gospel.

Matthew 7:6 In Context | *Jesus teaches a crowd of people about spiritual concepts.*

Jesus wanted people to understand that it is not wise to give what is holy or what is treasured to those who will not value or appreciate it.

10. *How can this same spiritual concept apply to God giving his Holy Spirit only to those who have committed to following Him through obedience of the gospel?*

Romans 8:6-18, 26-30 In Context | *Paul informs Christians of Rome about the work of the Spirit*

Study Reflections	Responses
11. *God cannot be pleased by those who live in or by what?*	

Study Reflections *(cont.)*	Responses
12. What does the Spirit testify or bear witness to Christians being?	
Read the information to the right. Then answer the question below.	In Romans chapter 8, Paul describes one of many different benefits of the Spirit found throughout scripture.
13. Reflection: Think of an experience you or someone you know has had that produced so much grief, pain, hurt, or sadness that it's often difficult to describe in words.	
14. According to Romans 8:26, in what ways can the Spirit provide help in situations like this?	

Exhibit E - Experience

Galatians 5:16-17, 22-26	In Context	*Paul informs Christians in Galatia about what the Spirit produces in a person.*

15. *What are, at least, three qualities Paul mentions that are eventually produced from possessing the Spirit?*

16. *In the next sections, describe how having each of these qualities can be beneficial and how lacking each can be destructive or unhealthy for individuals, families, and communities.*

Quality 1: _____

	Benefits of having this quality	*Disadvantages of lacking this quality*
Individuals:		
Families:		
Communities:		

Quality 2: _____

	Benefits of having this quality	*Disadvantages of lacking this quality*
Individuals:		
Families:		
Communities:		

Quality 3: _____

	Benefits of having this quality	*Disadvantages of lacking this quality*
Individuals:		
Families:		
Communities:		

Devotion 12: Evidently Present

> ". . . God, with an intimate knowledge of who we are, often seeks to convict us of who He is through the experiences we have."

*Read the passages, and answer the questions below.

Luke 5:1-11 — In Context | *Jesus selects the first apostles.*

Study Reflections	Responses
Read the statement to the right. Then answer the question below.	*Simon Peter and his companions were experienced fisherman who hadn't caught any fish after working hard all night.*
1. How does the passage describe their reaction to the great quantity of fish they caught by listening to Jesus?	
2. What was Peter's individual response to Jesus?	

Study Reflections *(cont.)*	Responses
3. What does Peter's response say about his perception of who Jesus was?	

Challenge Questions	Responses
4. What do you think led Peter to this perception about Jesus?	
5. What does this passage say about how God can use our experiences to help us establish faith in Him?	

Having been with Jesus for years and experiencing events like this would, no doubt, have strengthened the faith and trustworthiness of Jesus' message. In fact, both Peter and John – men present at this event – were always seeking to help others establish their belief in Christ, as well, by communicating what they had experienced as eyewitnesses of Jesus.

Exhibit E - Experience

6. Read 2 Peter 1:16. What did Peter write Christians about as it related to Christ?

7. Read 1 John 1:1-4. How did John describe the contact and interaction he had with Jesus to the Christians he wrote?

| Acts 4:1-20 | In Context | The apostles, Peter and John, are questioned about healing a man. |

8. In verse 13, what did those who questioned Peter and John begin to realize?

9. What did the men ask Peter and John to do in verse 18?

10. How did Peter and John answer these men in verses 19-20?

Even though Peter and John did not have formal religious training by the standard of that day and age, they were still able to answer and amaze those who were considered to be religious scholars because of the intimate experiences they had with Jesus. And for those of us who have obeyed the gospel and received the Spirit; we, too, can enjoy all the benefits that come with knowing God and his Son, Jesus Christ, very intimately – benefits that extend well beyond what we're able to understand with our intellect and wisdom alone. As the apostle, Paul, appropriately stressed, *"...my message and preaching were not in persuasive words of wisdom, but in demonstration of the Spirit and of power; so that your faith would not rest on the wisdom of men, but on the power of God." (1 Corinthians 2:4-5)*

Acts 16:25-34	In Context	*Paul and his companion, Silas, are imprisoned for teaching and advocating Jesus.*

Study Reflections	Responses
Read the statement to the right. Then answer the question below.	*The jailer understood that the consequence for escaped prisoners in that culture and time was normally death.*
11. What was the jailer about to do when he saw the prison doors opened?	

Exhibit E - Experience

Study Reflections *(cont.)*	Responses
12. *According to the passage, how many prisoners escaped?*	
13. *What question did the jailer ask Paul and Silas?*	
14. *How did Paul and Silas answer the jailer?*	
15. *What did the jailer do for Paul and Silas and for himself?*	

Challenge Questions	Responses
16. *What extraordinary events occurred in this passage that may have influenced the jailer to learn about and convert to Christianity, along with his entire household?*	

Challenge Questions *(cont.)*	Responses
17. What clues can this passage offer us about how God uses our experiences to confirm His presence and existence in our lives?	

Notes

PREFACE

1. Revelation 2:9
2. "Age-of-the-sage.org," accessed November 13, 2012, http://www.age-of-the-sage.org/quotations/marx_opium_people.html.

SECTION ONE: NOTHING LIKE THE REAL THING

1. Norman Giesler & William Nix, *From God to Us: How We got our Bible* (Chicago: Moody Bible Institute, 2012), 7.
2. Revelation 2:8
3. Isaiah 44:6-7
4. Isaiah 44:10-11, 24
5. Mark 9:3-6
6. Mark 9:7-8
7. Colossians 2:23
8. Galatians 5:19-21
9. 1 Corinthians 11:1
10. John 14:6
11. Galatians 1:6
12. 1 Corinthians 15:3-4

13. Galatians 1:10
14. John 6:67-69
15. Acts 4:12

SECTION TWO: DESTINED FOR EACH OTHER

1. Revelation 2:8
2. Lee Strobel, *The Case for the Resurrection: Investigating the Evidence for Belief* (Grand Rapids:Zondervan, 2009), 9.
3. Lee Strobel, *The Case for the Resurrection: Investigating the Evidence for Belief* (Grand Rapids:Zondervan, 2009), 10.
4. Lee Strobel, *The Case for the Resurrection: Investigating the Evidence for Belief* (Grand Rapids:Zondervan, 2009), 9.
5. Ecclesiastes 2:3-11
6. Jeremiah 10:23
7. Lee Strobel, *The Case for the Resurrection: Investigating the Evidence for Belief* (Grand Rapids:Zondervan, 2009), 11.
8. Ephesians 1:4-5
9. Ephesians 1:7
10. Isaiah 59:2
11. 1 Corinthians 15:1-4

12. "*The Real Jesus of History*," accessed November 13, 2012, http://www.doesgodexist.org/Pamphlets/TheRealJesusofHistory/TheRealJesusOfHistory.html.
13. "*The Real Jesus of History*," accessed November 13, 2012, http://www.doesgodexist.org/Pamphlets/TheRealJesusofHistory/TheRealJesusOfHistory.html.
14. "*Why I left Atheism*," accessed November 13, 2012, http://www.doesgodexist.org/AboutClayton/PastLife.html
15. Hebrews 11:1
16. Hebrews 11:6
17. Romans 6:3-4, 6, 12

Literature on the Bible

1. *A General Introduction to the Bible* by Norman Geisler & William Nix

2. *From God to Us: How We got our Bible* by Norman Geisler & William Nix

3. *God Wrote a Book* by James Macdonald

4. *How We Got the Bible* by Neil R. Lightfoot

5. *How We Got the Bible: A Visual Journey* by Clinton E. Arnold

6. *The Historical Reliability of the Gospels* by Craig Blomberg

7. *The Journey from Texts to Translations: The Origin and Development of the Bible* by Paul D. Wegner

8. *The New Testament Documents: Are they reliable?* by F.F. Bruce

9. *Who Wrote the Bible* by Richard Elliot Freeman

www.ingramcontent.com/pod-product-compliance
Lightning Source LLC
Chambersburg PA
CBHW080251170426
43192CB00014BA/2636